*To everyone who believes we can achieve our dreams
in unexpected ways —D.A.K.*

For my beautiful wife and newborn —O.D.

The author wishes to extend a special thanks to Jim Bintliff, owner of Lena
Blackburne Baseball Rubbing Mud, for his willingness to share his knowledge.

Text copyright © 2013 by David A. Kelly
Illustrations copyright © 2013 by Oliver Dominguez

Millbrook Press
A division of Lerner Publishing Group, Inc.
241 First Avenue North
Minneapolis, MN 55401 U.S.A.

Website address: www.lernerbooks.com

Main body text set in Cheltenham ITC Std Book 20/30.
Typeface provided by International Tyepface Corp.

Library of Congress Cataloging-in-Publication Data

Kelly, David A. (David Andrew), 1964–
    Miracle mud : Lena Blackburne and the secret mud that changed baseball / by
David A. Kelly ; illustrated by Oliver Dominguez.
        p.   cm.
    ISBN: 978–0–7613–8092–4 (lib. bdg. : alk. paper)
    1. Blackburne, Lena, 1886–1968—Juvenile literature. 2. Baseball players—United
States—Biography—Juvenile literature. 3. Inventors—United States—Biography—
Juvenile literature. 4. Baseball—United States—Equipment and supplies—Juvenile
literature. 5. Sports—United States—Marketing—Juvenile literature. I. Dominguez,
Oliver. II. Title.
GV865.B552A3 2013
796.357092—dc23 [B]   2012020917

Manufactured in the United States of America
1 – DP – 12/31/12

MIRACLE MUD

LENA BLACKBURNE AND THE SECRET MUD THAT CHANGED BASEBALL

David A. Kelly

illustrated by

Oliver Dominguez

M Millbrook Press / Minneapolis

Lena Blackburne wanted to be a famous baseball player.

But instead, he discovered mud. Baseball mud. His special, secret mud changed the game of baseball.

Lena didn't set
out to find mud.

He just wanted to be a
great baseball player...

But he wasn't.

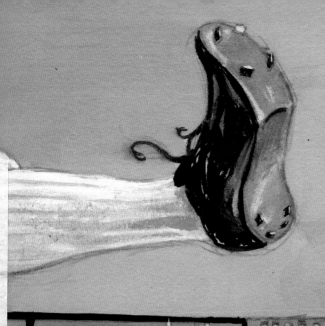

Starting in 1910, Lena played for lots
of baseball teams. He played first base,
second base, third base, and shortstop.

He even pitched in one game.

No matter how hard he tried, he wasn't good enough to become a star like Cy Young or Babe Ruth.

He wasn't going to be
in the Hall of Fame.

When his playing days were over,
Lena became a coach.

One day, an umpire complained to
Lena about the baseballs. They were
too wet and soft. The soggy balls
were hard for pitchers to throw.
They were hard for batters to see.
And they were hard to hit very far.

The umpire was right.
The balls were a mess.

Brand-new baseballs were too shiny and slick. So players soaked them in dirty water. It got rid of the shine. But it also made the balls soggy and soft.

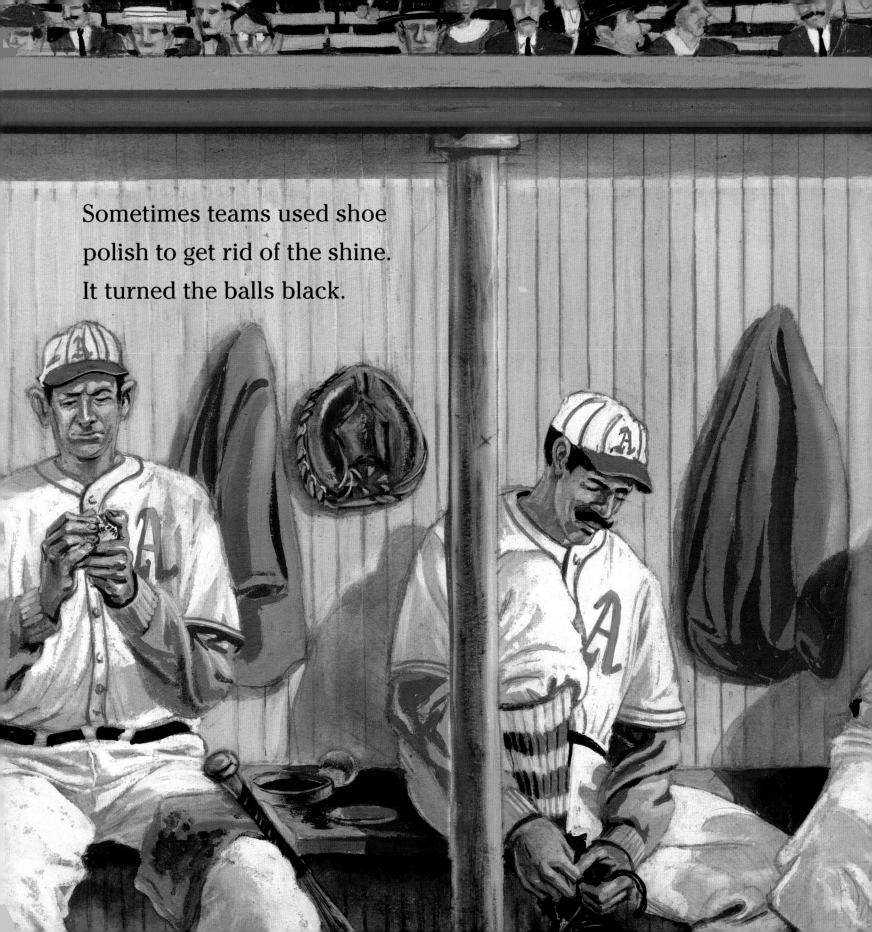

Sometimes teams used shoe
polish to get rid of the shine.
It turned the balls black.

Players even rubbed balls with spit and tobacco juice. That made the balls stink.

"There has to be a better way,"
Lena said.

But where would he look? What
would take the shine off the balls
without hurting them?

The next time Lena was home, he went to an old fishing hole. He lived near a river in New Jersey.

Sploooootch! He stepped into some dark brown mud. It was soft and gooey. Lena's boot stuck in the mud. He slooooooooowly pulled it out.

Lena had an idea.

He reached down and scooped up some of the dark brown mud. It looked smooth and creamy like chocolate pudding. But it felt gritty.

Lena took the mud to the ballpark. He rubbed it on some baseballs and let it dry. Then he wiped them with a cloth. The powdered mud came off easily.

The shine was gone! And the balls weren't black or dirty.
They didn't smell. They weren't even soft.

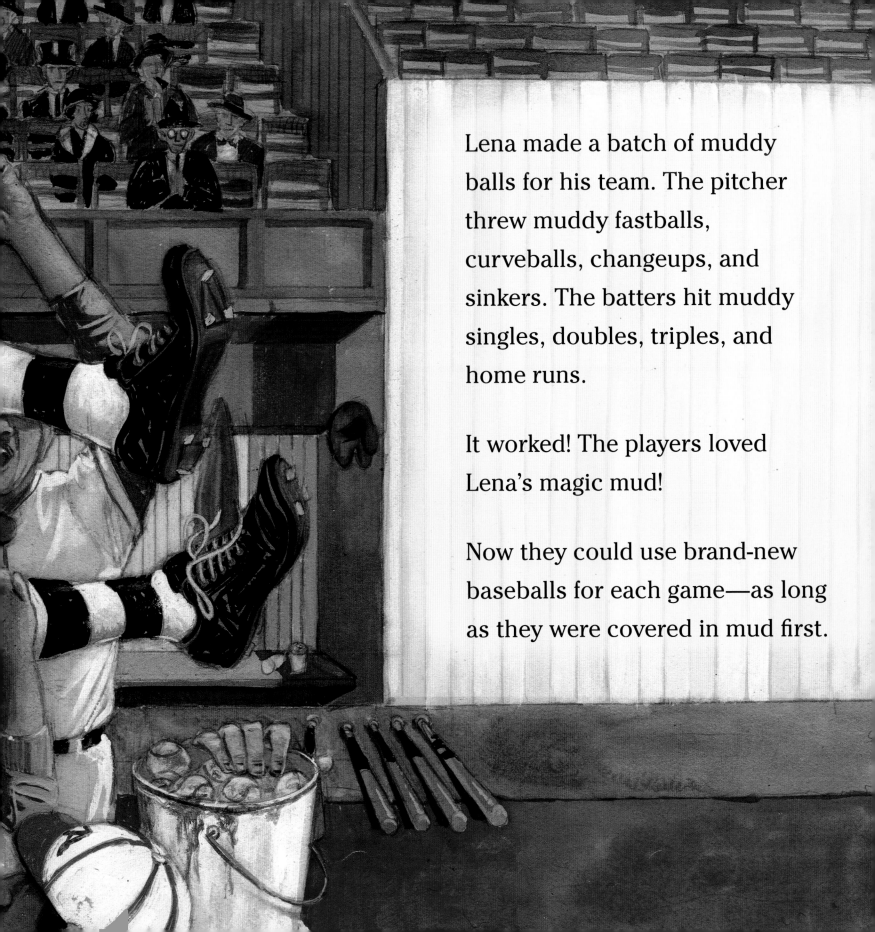

Lena made a batch of muddy balls for his team. The pitcher threw muddy fastballs, curveballs, changeups, and sinkers. The batters hit muddy singles, doubles, triples, and home runs.

It worked! The players loved Lena's magic mud!

Now they could use brand-new baseballs for each game—as long as they were covered in mud first.

Lena went back for more mud. He put it into tubs and started selling it. Lots of teams bought Lena Blackburne's Baseball Rubbing Mud.

Lena became a "mud farmer." He never told anyone where he got the baseball mud. It was a secret.

But it was no secret that the mud worked. Baseball teams have been buying tubs of Lena's mud for close to seventy-five years. That's millions and millions of muddy baseballs.

Lena's mud is the only thing that's allowed on major-league balls. Players can't use water or spit or shoe polish. Just mud. Lena's mud.

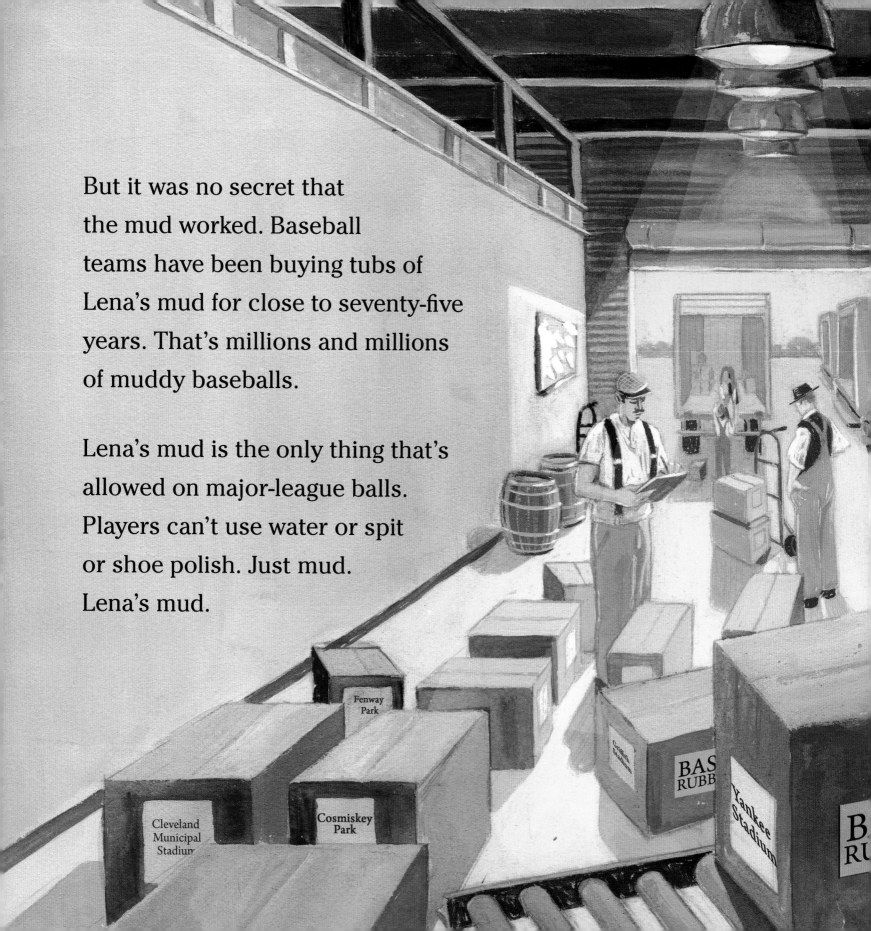

Lena Blackburne didn't make it into the Baseball Hall of Fame. But his mud did. In 1969, a tub of his magic mud was put on display in the Baseball Hall of Fame.

Now, every spring,
teams have crisp
new uniforms.
Brand-new bats.
Squeaky-clean cleats.

And thanks to Lena,
lots and lots of mud!

Author's Note

Dirty baseballs have been around since baseball was born. At first, baseball teams used baseballs for as long as they could. Sometimes they would use just one ball for an entire game. The more a baseball had been used, the easier it was for the pitchers to nick it and scuff it. Nicks and scuffs made the balls unpredictable. That made them harder for batters to hit. But it also made them dangerous. Ray Chapman, a shortstop for the Cleveland Indians, was killed when he was struck by an erratic baseball in a game on August 16, 1920.

After that, umpires tried to replace damaged balls during games with new baseballs. But the leather on new baseballs is smooth, slick, and shiny, making it difficult for pitchers to get a good grip. The bright white cover also reflects light, making it hard for batters to see the ball well. So players started using everything from shoe polish to dirt to tobacco juice (saliva mixed with the juice of tobacco leaves from wads of chewing tobacco) to make balls dirty. Nothing worked very well.

Russell Aubrey "Lena" Blackburne played Major League Baseball for eight years, mostly for the Chicago White Sox. He also played short periods for the Cincinnati Reds, the Boston Braves, and the Philadelphia Phillies. Blackburne was a rather ordinary infielder. But he was good enough to become a coach. The Philadelphia Athletics hired Lena to be their third base coach in 1933. It was during this time that an umpire complained about the messy, soggy balls they had to use for games.

LENA BLACKBURNE STATS

- Born: Oct 23, 1886, Clifton Heights, Pennsylvania
- Died: Feb 29, 1968, Riverside, New Jersey
- Played in 550 major league games over eight years
- Hit 4 home runs
- .214 batting average
- Height: 5'11"
- Weight: 160

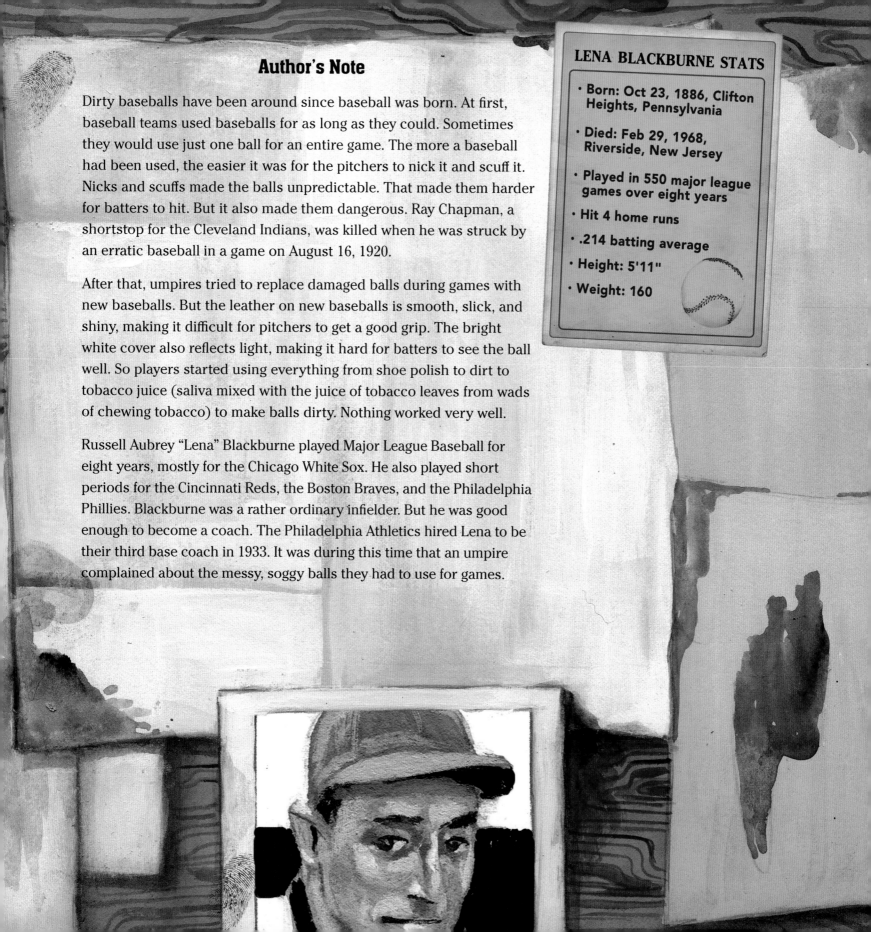

Lena discovered his special mud near his home in New Jersey, along the banks of the Delaware River. He started selling it in 1938. At first, Lena only sold the mud to American League teams because he was an American League fan. By the 1950s, he was selling it to National League teams as well.

Lena continued to supply teams with mud until his death in 1968. In his will, Lena left the business to one of his friends, John Haas, who had helped Lena harvest mud. Haas passed the mud farming business on to his son-in-law, Burns Bintliff. Later on, Burns's son Jim Bintliff took over. Today, Jim Bintliff owns the business.

The official rules of Major League Baseball (Rule 3.01 (c)) require that before a game, the umpire should, among other things, ensure the baseballs to be used are regulation baseballs and "that they are properly rubbed so that the gloss is removed." One of the home team's clubhouse attendants typically takes care of rubbing about seventy-two balls with mud before each game.

While baseball mud is used during every game from spring training to the World Series, the mud harvesting season starts in July. Jim and his crew take a boat out to their secret mud hole. They scoop up hundreds of pounds of mud and bring it back to shore. Then comes the super-secret part: they store the mucky brown mud in barrels over the winter. Perhaps something special happens in the barrels. We don't know. And they won't tell.